RED FOX VS. FISHER

BY NATHAN SOMMER

BELLWETHER MEDIA • MINNEAPOLIS, MN

Torque brims with excitement
perfect for thrill-seekers of all kinds.
Discover daring survival skills, explore
uncharted worlds, and marvel at mighty
engines and extreme sports. In *Torque* books,
anything can happen. Are you ready?

This edition first published in 2024 by Bellwether Media, Inc.

No part of this publication may be reproduced in whole or in part without written
permission of the publisher. For information regarding permission, write to
Bellwether Media, Inc., Attention: Permissions Department,
6012 Blue Circle Drive, Minnetonka, MN 55343.

Library of Congress Cataloging-in-Publication Data

LC record for Red Fox vs. Fisher available at: https://lccn.loc.gov/2023042534

Text copyright © 2024 by Bellwether Media, Inc. TORQUE and associated logos
are trademarks and/or registered trademarks of Bellwether Media, Inc.

Editor: Suzane Nguyen   Designer: Josh Brink

Printed in the United States of America, North Mankato, MN.

TABLE OF CONTENTS

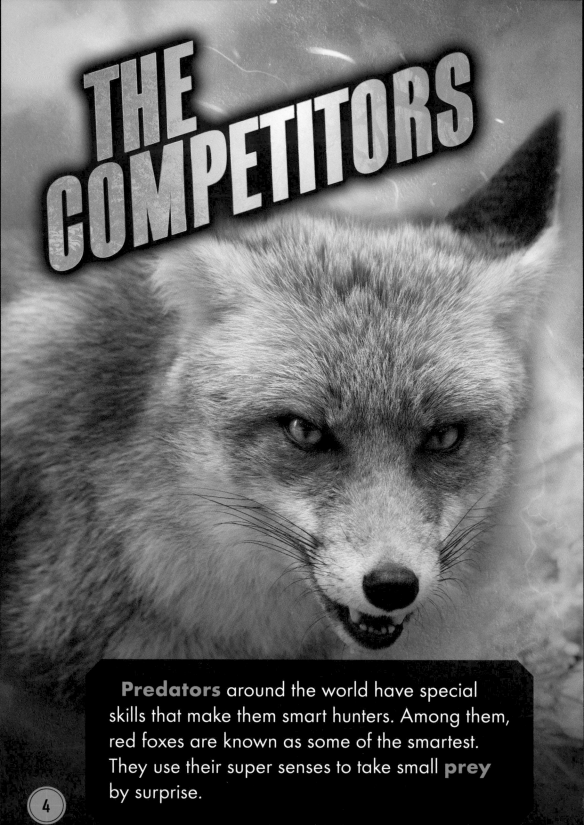

THE COMPETITORS

Predators around the world have special skills that make them smart hunters. Among them, red foxes are known as some of the smartest. They use their super senses to take small **prey** by surprise.

Fishers are worthy **rivals** to red foxes. These **agile** hunters are hard to escape on the ground and in the treetops. Which of these smart hunters would win in a battle?

RED FOX PROFILE

LENGTH
UP TO 4.6 FEET
(1.4 METERS)

WEIGHT
UP TO 24 POUNDS
(11 KILOGRAMS)

0	2 FEET	4 FEET	6 FEET

HABITAT

 FORESTS

GRASSLANDS

 MOUNTAINS

 DESERTS

RED FOX RANGE

■ RANGE

Red foxes are the largest and most widespread foxes in the world. Most have thick, reddish-brown fur with white underbellies. The foxes have long black legs and large, bushy tails.

Red foxes **adapt** to many **habitats**. They are found in forests, grasslands, mountains, and deserts. The **mammals** live in underground dens.

FOX DENS

The largest red fox dens can be up to 75 feet (23 meters) long!

Fishers are large members of the weasel family. These mammals have narrow bodies with short legs and long, furry tails. The largest can grow up to 3.5 feet (1.1 meters) long from head to tail.

Fishers usually live alone. They prefer to live in thick forests. Fishers make dens in trees or under rocks and logs.

FISHER PROFILE

LENGTH
UP TO 3.5 FEET
(1.1 METERS)

WEIGHT
UP TO 20 POUNDS
(9.1 KILOGRAMS)

| 0 | 1 FOOT | 2 FEET | 3 FEET | 4 FEET |

HABITAT

FORESTS

WOODLANDS

FISHER RANGE

□ RANGE

SECRET WEAPONS

Fishers are built to climb. Sharp, **retractable** claws help them climb trees quickly. These agile hunters can catch squirrels and other prey in the branches of trees.

PORCUPINE PREDATORS

Fishers are one of the porcupine's main predators. They avoid the porcupine's quills by attacking its face.

RED FOX HEARING

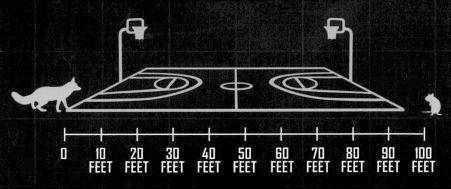

BASKETBALL COURT: 94 FEET (29 METERS)

FOX HEARING A MOUSE SQUEAK: 100 FEET (30.5 METERS)

| 0 | 10 FEET | 20 FEET | 30 FEET | 40 FEET | 50 FEET | 60 FEET | 70 FEET | 80 FEET | 90 FEET | 100 FEET |

Red foxes use great hearing to find prey. They can hear a mouse squeaking 100 feet (30.5 meters) away. The foxes also find mice moving underground.

Long legs help red foxes leap up to 15 feet (4.6 meters) in one bound. They are silent when they pounce. Most small prey cannot escape them!

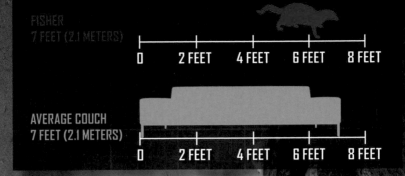

FISHER
7 FEET (2.1 METERS)

| 0 | 2 FEET | 4 FEET | 6 FEET | 8 FEET |

AVERAGE COUCH
7 FEET (2.1 METERS)

| 0 | 2 FEET | 4 FEET | 6 FEET | 8 FEET |

Strong back legs help fishers climb down trees headfirst. This allows them to attack prey from above! Their legs also help them jump up to 7 feet (2.1 meters) between trees.

13

SECRET WEAPONS

RED FOX

GREAT HEARING

LONG LEGS

SHARP TEETH

Red foxes have rows of sharp teeth. They attack by biting the head and neck of prey many times. The foxes can even tear off fur and feathers of animals with their teeth!

SHARP CLAWS

STRONG LEGS

SHARP TEETH

Fishers have sharp teeth, too. They defeat prey with deadly bites to the head and neck. Their bites can take down animals double their size!

ATTACK MOVES

Red foxes are mostly **nocturnal** hunters. They use sound to hunt. The foxes silently wait once they hear prey. They listen to find their prey's exact location. Then, the foxes pounce!

Fishers find most prey by smell.
They often catch prey by surprise.
Then, they chase it into trees or tight areas
underground. After that, the attack begins!

THE WHOLE THING

Fishers do not waste their
meals. They often leave
behind only a pile of bones!

Red foxes leap and pin their prey down. Sometimes they chase their meal. The foxes defeat prey with bites to the head and neck.

DUCK HUNTERS

Red foxes kill around one million wild ducks each year in North America!

Fishers slow prey down with multiple bites to the face. Then they **lunge** at the necks and underbellies of hurt prey.

READY, FIGHT!

A red fox prepares to **ambush** a mouse. Suddenly, a fisher exits the tall grass nearby. The fisher bites the fox before it can attack its prey.

The fox snaps back at the fisher.
It runs underground. But the fisher follows.
The fisher defeats the trapped fox with
more bites. The fierce fisher won today!

GLOSSARY

adapt—to get used to different conditions easily

agile—able to move quickly and easily

ambush—to carry out a surprise attack

habitats—the homes or areas where animals prefer to live

lunge—to move forward quickly

mammals—warm-blooded animals that have backbones and feed their young milk

nocturnal—active at night

predators—animals that hunt other animals for food

prey—animals that are hunted by other animals for food

retractable—able to be pulled back in

rivals—animals that compete for the same thing as other animals

TO LEARN MORE

AT THE LIBRARY

Downs, Kieran. *Wolverine vs. Honey Badger.* Minneapolis, Minn.: Bellwether Media, 2021.

Lombardo, Jennifer. *Foxes in the Forest.* New York, N.Y.: Gareth Stevens Publishing, 2023.

Sommer, Nathan. *Arctic Fox vs. Snowy Owl.* Minneapolis, Minn.: Bellwether Media, 2024.

ON THE WEB

FACTSURFER

Factsurfer.com gives you a safe, fun way to find more information.

1. Go to www.factsurfer.com

2. Enter "red fox vs. fisher" into the search box and click 🔍.

3. Select your book cover to see a list of related content.

INDEX